This sweary
2022-2023
planner
belongs to:

_____

PERSONAL *Information*

NAME
_____

ADDRESS
_____

CITY _____ STATE _____

HOME _____ CELL _____

EMAIL
_____

COMPANY NAME
_____

ADDRESS
_____

CITY _____ STATE _____

PHONE _____ CELL _____

EMAIL
_____

DOCTOR
_____

DENTIST
_____

ALLERGIES
_____

BLOOD TYPE
_____

ESSENTIAL INFORMATION
_____

EMERGENCY
_____

NOTIFY & RELATIONSHIPS
_____

ADDRESS
_____

CITY _____ STATE _____

PHONE
_____

EMAIL
_____

2022

January

MON	TUE	WED	THU	FRI	SAT	SUN
					1	2
3	4	5	6	7	8	9
10	11	12	13	14	15	16
17	18	19	20	21	22	23
24	25	26	27	28	29	30
31						

February

MON	TUE	WED	THU	FRI	SAT	SUN
	1	2	3	4	5	6
7	8	9	10	11	12	13
14	15	16	17	18	19	20
21	22	23	24	25	26	27
28						

March

MON	TUE	WED	THU	FRI	SAT	SUN
	1	2	3	4	5	6
7	8	9	10	11	12	13
14	15	16	17	18	19	20
21	22	23	24	25	26	27
28	29	30	31			

April

MON	TUE	WED	THU	FRI	SAT	SUN
				1	2	3
4	5	6	7	8	9	10
11	12	13	14	15	16	17
18	19	20	21	22	23	24
25	26	27	28	29	30	

May

MON	TUE	WED	THU	FRI	SAT	SUN
						1
2	3	4	5	6	7	8
9	10	11	12	13	14	15
16	17	18	19	20	21	22
23	24	25	26	27	28	29
30	31					

June

MON	TUE	WED	THU	FRI	SAT	SUN
		1	2	3	4	5
6	7	8	9	10	11	12
13	14	15	16	17	18	19
20	21	22	23	24	25	26
27	28	29	30			

July

MON	TUE	WED	THU	FRI	SAT	SUN
				1	2	3
4	5	6	7	8	9	10
11	12	13	14	15	16	17
18	19	20	21	22	23	24
25	26	27	28	29	30	31

August

MON	TUE	WED	THU	FRI	SAT	SUN
1	2	3	4	5	6	7
8	9	10	11	12	13	14
15	16	17	18	19	20	21
22	23	24	25	26	27	28
29	30	31				

September

MON	TUE	WED	THU	FRI	SAT	SUN
			1	2	3	4
5	6	7	8	9	10	11
12	13	14	15	16	17	18
19	20	21	22	23	24	25
26	27	28	29	30		

October

MON	TUE	WED	THU	FRI	SAT	SUN
					1	2
3	4	5	6	7	8	9
10	11	12	13	14	15	16
17	18	19	20	21	22	23
24	25	26	27	28	29	30
31						

November

MON	TUE	WED	THU	FRI	SAT	SUN
	1	2	3	4	5	6
7	8	9	10	11	12	13
14	15	16	17	18	19	20
21	22	23	24	25	26	27
28	29	30				

December

MON	TUE	WED	THU	FRI	SAT	SUN
			1	2	3	4
5	6	7	8	9	10	11
12	13	14	15	16	17	18
19	20	21	22	23	24	25
26	27	28	29	30	31	

2023

January

MON	TUE	WED	THU	FRI	SAT	SUN
						1
2	3	4	5	6	7	8
9	10	11	12	13	14	15
16	17	18	19	20	21	22
23	24	25	26	27	28	29
30	31					

February

MON	TUE	WED	THU	FRI	SAT	SUN
		1	2	3	4	5
6	7	8	9	10	11	12
13	14	15	16	17	18	19
20	21	22	23	24	25	26
27	28					

March

MON	TUE	WED	THU	FRI	SAT	SUN
		1	2	3	4	5
6	7	8	9	10	11	12
13	14	15	16	17	18	19
20	21	22	23	24	25	26
27	28	29	30	31		

April

MON	TUE	WED	THU	FRI	SAT	SUN
					1	2
3	4	5	6	7	8	9
10	11	12	13	14	15	16
17	18	19	20	21	22	23
24	25	26	27	28	29	30

May

MON	TUE	WED	THU	FRI	SAT	SUN
1	2	3	4	5	6	7
8	9	10	11	12	13	14
15	16	17	18	19	20	21
22	23	24	25	26	27	28
29	30	31				

June

MON	TUE	WED	THU	FRI	SAT	SUN
			1	2	3	4
5	6	7	8	9	10	11
12	13	14	15	16	17	18
19	20	21	22	23	24	25
26	27	28	29	30		

July

MON	TUE	WED	THU	FRI	SAT	SUN
					1	2
3	4	5	6	7	8	9
10	11	12	13	14	15	16
17	18	19	20	21	22	23
24	25	26	27	28	29	30
31						

August

MON	TUE	WED	THU	FRI	SAT	SUN
	1	2	3	4	5	6
7	8	9	10	11	12	13
14	15	16	17	18	19	20
21	22	23	24	25	26	27
28	29	30	31			

September

MON	TUE	WED	THU	FRI	SAT	SUN
				1	2	3
4	5	6	7	8	9	10
11	12	13	14	15	16	17
18	19	20	21	22	23	24
25	26	27	28	29	30	

October

MON	TUE	WED	THU	FRI	SAT	SUN
						1
2	3	4	5	6	7	8
9	10	11	12	13	14	15
16	17	18	19	20	21	22
23	24	25	26	27	28	29
30	31					

November

MON	TUE	WED	THU	FRI	SAT	SUN
		1	2	3	4	5
6	7	8	9	10	11	12
13	14	15	16	17	18	19
20	21	22	23	24	25	26
27	28	29	30			

December

MON	TUE	WED	THU	FRI	SAT	SUN
				1	2	3
4	5	6	7	8	9	10
11	12	13	14	15	16	17
18	19	20	21	22	23	24
25	26	27	28	29	30	31

2022

GOALS FOR 2022:

2022

January

MON	TUE	WED	THU	FRI	SAT	SUN
					1	2
3	4	5	6	7	8	9
10	11	12	13	14	15	16
17	18	19	20	21	22	23
24	25	26	27	28	29	30
31						

February

MON	TUE	WED	THU	FRI	SAT	SUN
	1	2	3	4	5	6
7	8	9	10	11	12	13
14	15	16	17	18	19	20
21	22	23	24	25	26	27
28						

March

MON	TUE	WED	THU	FRI	SAT	SUN
	1	2	3	4	5	6
7	8	9	10	11	12	13
14	15	16	17	18	19	20
21	22	23	24	25	26	27
28	29	30	31			

April

MON	TUE	WED	THU	FRI	SAT	SUN
				1	2	3
4	5	6	7	8	9	10
11	12	13	14	15	16	17
18	19	20	21	22	23	24
25	26	27	28	29	30	

May

MON	TUE	WED	THU	FRI	SAT	SUN
						1
2	3	4	5	6	7	8
9	10	11	12	13	14	15
16	17	18	19	20	21	22
23	24	25	26	27	28	29
30	31					

June

MON	TUE	WED	THU	FRI	SAT	SUN
		1	2	3	4	5
6	7	8	9	10	11	12
13	14	15	16	17	18	19
20	21	22	23	24	25	26
27	28	29	30			

Notes

_____

_____

_____

_____

_____

_____

_____

_____

_____

2022

July

MON	TUE	WED	THU	FRI	SAT	SUN
				1	2	3
4	5	6	7	8	9	10
11	12	13	14	15	16	17
18	19	20	21	22	23	24
25	26	27	28	29	30	31

August

MON	TUE	WED	THU	FRI	SAT	SUN
1	2	3	4	5	6	7
8	9	10	11	12	13	14
15	16	17	18	19	20	21
22	23	24	25	26	27	28
29	30	31				

September

MON	TUE	WED	THU	FRI	SAT	SUN
			1	2	3	4
5	6	7	8	9	10	11
12	13	14	15	16	17	18
19	20	21	22	23	24	25
26	27	28	29	30		

October

MON	TUE	WED	THU	FRI	SAT	SUN
					1	2
3	4	5	6	7	8	9
10	11	12	13	14	15	16
17	18	19	20	21	22	23
24	25	26	27	28	29	30
31						

November

MON	TUE	WED	THU	FRI	SAT	SUN
	1	2	3	4	5	6
7	8	9	10	11	12	13
14	15	16	17	18	19	20
21	22	23	24	25	26	27
28	29	30				

December

MON	TUE	WED	THU	FRI	SAT	SUN
			1	2	3	4
5	6	7	8	9	10	11
12	13	14	15	16	17	18
19	20	21	22	23	24	25
26	27	28	29	30	31	

Notes

_____

_____

_____

_____

_____

_____

_____

_____

_____

_____

January

2022

MONTHLY GOALS

MONTHLY SNAPSHOT

TOP PRIORITIES

TASKS & NOTES

Shit to Get Done This Month

TASK/PROJECT	DUE DATE
○	
○	
○	
○	
○	
○	
○	
○	
○	
○	
○	
○	
○	
○	
○	
○	
○	
○	
○	
○	
○	
○	
○	
○	
○	

January 2022

MONDAY	TUESDAY	WEDNESDAY	THURSDAY
27	28	29	30
3	4	5	6
10	11	12	13
17	18	19	20
24	25	26	27
31	1	2	3

January 2022

FRIDAY	SATURDAY	SUNDAY	Notes
	1	2	
7	8	9	
14	15	16	
21	22	23	
28	29	30	
4	5	6	

Shit To Do

_____

_____

_____

_____

_____

_____

_____

_____

_____

_____

_____

_____

_____

_____

_____

_____

_____

_____

_____

_____

_____

_____

_____

Shit To Do

_____

_____

_____

_____

_____

_____

_____

_____

_____

_____

_____

_____

_____

_____

_____

_____

_____

_____

_____

_____

_____

_____

Shit To Do

_____
_____
_____
_____
_____
_____
_____
_____
_____
_____
_____
_____
_____
_____
_____
_____
_____
_____
_____
_____
_____
_____

February

2022

MONTHLY GOALS

MONTHLY SNAPSHOT

TOP PRIORITIES

TASKS & NOTES

Shit to Get Done This Month

TASK/PROJECT	DUE DATE
○	
○	
○	
○	
○	
○	
○	
○	
○	
○	
○	
○	
○	
○	
○	
○	
○	
○	
○	
○	
○	
○	
○	
○	
○	
○	
○	

TASK/PROJECT	DUE DATE

February 2022

MONDAY	TUESDAY	WEDNESDAY	THURSDAY
	1	2	3
7	8	9	10
14	15	16	17
21	22	23	24
28			

February

2022

FRIDAY	SATURDAY	SUNDAY	Notes
4	5	6	
11	12	13	
18	19	20	
25	26	27	

Shit To Do

_____

_____

_____

_____

_____

_____

_____

_____

_____

_____

_____

_____

_____

_____

_____

_____

_____

_____

_____

_____

_____

_____

_____

Shit To Do

_____

_____

_____

_____

_____

_____

_____

_____

_____

_____

_____

_____

_____

_____

_____

_____

_____

_____

_____

_____

Shit To Do

_____
_____
_____
_____
_____
_____
_____
_____
_____
_____
_____
_____
_____
_____
_____
_____
_____
_____
_____
_____
_____
_____

March

2022

MONTHLY GOALS

MONTHLY SNAPSHOT

TOP PRIORITIES

TASKS & NOTES

Shit to Get Done This Month

TASK/PROJECT	DUE DATE
○	
○	
○	
○	
○	
○	
○	
○	
○	
○	
○	
○	
○	
○	
○	
○	
○	
○	
○	
○	
○	
○	
○	
○	

March

2022

MONDAY	TUESDAY	WEDNESDAY	THURSDAY
28	1	2	3
7	8	9	10
14	15	16	17
21	22	23	24
28	29	30	31

March
2022

FRIDAY	SATURDAY	SUNDAY	Notes
4	5	6	
11	12	13	
18	19	20	
25	26	27	

Shit To Do

_____
_____
_____
_____
_____
_____
_____
_____
_____
_____
_____
_____
_____
_____
_____
_____
_____
_____
_____
_____
_____
_____
_____

Shit To Do

_____
_____
_____
_____
_____
_____
_____
_____
_____
_____
_____
_____
_____
_____
_____
_____
_____
_____
_____
_____
_____
_____
_____
_____

Shit To Do

April

2022

MONTHLY GOALS

MONTHLY SNAPSHOT

TOP PRIORITIES

TASKS & NOTES

Shit to Get Done This Month

TASK/PROJECT	DUE DATE
○	
○	
○	
○	
○	
○	
○	
○	
○	
○	
○	
○	
○	
○	
○	
○	
○	
○	
○	
○	
○	
○	
○	
○	
○	

April | 2022

MONDAY	TUESDAY	WEDNESDAY	THURSDAY
4	5	6	7
11	12	13	14
18	19	20	21
25	26	27	28

April

2022

FRIDAY	SATURDAY	SUNDAY	Notes
1	2	3	
8	9	10	
15	16	17	
22	23	24	
29	30		

Shit To Do

_____

_____

_____

_____

_____

_____

_____

_____

_____

_____

_____

_____

_____

_____

_____

_____

_____

_____

_____

_____

_____

Shit To Do

_____
_____
_____
_____
_____
_____
_____
_____
_____
_____
_____
_____
_____
_____
_____
_____
_____
_____
_____
_____
_____
_____
_____
_____
_____
_____

Shit To Do

_____

_____

_____

_____

_____

_____

_____

_____

_____

_____

_____

_____

_____

_____

_____

_____

_____

_____

May

2022

MONTHLY GOALS

MONTHLY SNAPSHOT

TOP PRIORITIES

TASKS & NOTES

Shit to Get Done This Month

TASK/PROJECT	DUE DATE
○	
○	
○	
○	
○	
○	
○	
○	
○	
○	
○	
○	
○	
○	
○	
○	
○	
○	
○	
○	
○	
○	
○	
○	
○	
○	

TASK/PROJECT	DUE DATE

May

2022

MONDAY	TUESDAY	WEDNESDAY	THURSDAY
25	26	27	28
2	3	4	5
9	10	11	12
16	17	18	19
23	24	25	26
30	31	1	2

May

2022

FRIDAY	SATURDAY	SUNDAY	Notes
29	30	1	
6	7	8	
13	14	15	
20	21	22	
27	28	29	
3	4	5	

Shit To Do

_____
_____
_____
_____
_____
_____
_____
_____
_____
_____
_____
_____
_____
_____
_____
_____
_____
_____

Shit To Do

_____

_____

_____

_____

_____

_____

_____

_____

_____

_____

_____

_____

_____

_____

_____

_____

_____

_____

_____

_____

_____

_____

Shit To Do

June

2022

MONTHLY GOALS

MONTHLY SNAPSHOT

TOP PRIORITIES

TASKS & NOTES

Shit to Get Done This Month

TASK/PROJECT	DUE DATE
○	
○	
○	
○	
○	
○	
○	
○	
○	
○	
○	
○	
○	
○	
○	
○	
○	
○	
○	
○	
○	
○	
○	
○	

June 2022

MONDAY	TUESDAY	WEDNESDAY	THURSDAY
		1	2
6	7	8	9
13	14	15	16
20	21	22	23
27	28	29	30

June

2022

FRIDAY	SATURDAY	SUNDAY	Notes
3	4	5	
10	11	12	
17	18	19	
24	25	26	

Shit To Do

_____

_____

_____

_____

_____

_____

_____

_____

_____

_____

_____

_____

_____

_____

_____

_____

_____

_____

_____

_____

Shit To Do

_____

_____

_____

_____

_____

_____

_____

_____

_____

_____

_____

_____

_____

_____

_____

_____

_____

_____

_____

_____

_____

Shit To Do

July

2022

MONTHLY GOALS

MONTHLY SNAPSHOT

TOP PRIORITIES

TASKS & NOTES

Shit to Get Done This Month

TASK/PROJECT	DUE DATE
○	
○	
○	
○	
○	
○	
○	
○	
○	
○	
○	
○	
○	
○	
○	
○	
○	
○	
○	
○	
○	
○	
○	
○	
○	

July 2022

MONDAY	TUESDAY	WEDNESDAY	THURSDAY
27	28	29	30
4	5	6	7
11	12	13	14
18	19	20	21
25	26	27	28

July | 2022

FRIDAY	SATURDAY	SUNDAY	Notes
	1	2	3
8	9	10	
15	16	17	
22	23	24	
29	30	31	

Shit To Do

Shit To Do

_____
_____
_____
_____
_____
_____
_____
_____
_____
_____
_____
_____
_____
_____
_____
_____
_____
_____
_____
_____
_____
_____

Shit To Do

August

2022

MONTHLY GOALS

MONTHLY SNAPSHOT

TOP PRIORITIES

TASKS & NOTES

Shit to Get Done This Month

TASK/PROJECT	DUE DATE
○	
○	
○	
○	
○	
○	
○	
○	
○	
○	
○	
○	
○	
○	
○	
○	
○	
○	
○	
○	
○	
○	
○	
○	
○	
○	

August 2022

MONDAY	TUESDAY	WEDNESDAY	THURSDAY
1	2	3	4
8	9	10	11
15	16	17	18
22	23	24	25
29	30	31	

August 2022

FRIDAY	SATURDAY	SUNDAY	Notes
5	6	7	
12	13	14	
19	20	21	
26	27	28	

Shit To Do

_____
_____
_____
_____
_____
_____
_____
_____
_____
_____
_____
_____
_____
_____
_____
_____
_____
_____
_____
_____
_____

Shit To Do

_____
_____
_____
_____
_____
_____
_____
_____
_____
_____
_____
_____
_____
_____
_____
_____
_____
_____
_____
_____
_____
_____
_____

Shit To Do

_____

_____

_____

_____

_____

_____

_____

_____

_____

_____

_____

_____

_____

_____

_____

_____

_____

_____

_____

_____

September
2022

MONTHLY GOALS

MONTHLY SNAPSHOT

TOP PRIORITIES

TASKS & NOTES

Shit to Get Done This Month

TASK/PROJECT	DUE DATE
○	
○	
○	
○	
○	
○	
○	
○	
○	
○	
○	
○	
○	
○	
○	
○	
○	
○	
○	
○	
○	
○	
○	
○	

September 2022

MONDAY	TUESDAY	WEDNESDAY	THURSDAY
29	30	31	1
5	6	7	8
12	13	14	15
19	20	21	22
26	27	28	29

September 2022

FRIDAY	SATURDAY	SUNDAY	Notes
2	3	4	
9	10	11	
16	17	18	
23	24	25	
30			

Shit To Do

Shit To Do

_____

_____

_____

_____

_____

_____

_____

_____

_____

_____

_____

_____

_____

_____

_____

_____

_____

_____

_____

_____

_____

Shit To Do

_____

_____

_____

_____

_____

_____

_____

_____

_____

_____

_____

_____

_____

_____

_____

_____

_____

_____

_____

_____

_____

October

2022

MONTHLY GOALS

MONTHLY SNAPSHOT

TOP PRIORITIES

TASKS & NOTES

Shit to Get Done This Month

TASK/PROJECT	DUE DATE
⃝	
⃝	
⃝	
⃝	
⃝	
⃝	
⃝	
⃝	
⃝	
⃝	
⃝	
⃝	
⃝	
⃝	
⃝	
⃝	
⃝	
⃝	
⃝	
⃝	
⃝	
⃝	
⃝	
⃝	

October

2022

MONDAY	TUESDAY	WEDNESDAY	THURSDAY
3	4	5	6
10	11	12	13
17	18	19	20
24	25	26	27
31	1	2	3

October 2022

FRIDAY	SATURDAY	SUNDAY	Notes
30	1	2	
7	8	9	
14	15	16	
21	22	23	
28	29	30	
4	5	6	

Shit To Do

Shit To Do

_____
_____
_____
_____
_____
_____
_____
_____
_____
_____
_____
_____
_____
_____
_____
_____
_____
_____
_____
_____
_____
_____
_____

Shit To Do

_____

_____

_____

_____

_____

_____

_____

_____

_____

_____

_____

_____

_____

_____

_____

_____

_____

_____

_____

_____

_____

November

2022

MONTHLY GOALS

MONTHLY SNAPSHOT

TOP PRIORITIES

TASKS & NOTES

Shit to Get Done This Month

TASK/PROJECT	DUE DATE
○	
○	
○	
○	
○	
○	
○	
○	
○	
○	
○	
○	
○	
○	
○	
○	
○	
○	
○	
○	
○	
○	
○	
○	
○	

November 2022

MONDAY	TUESDAY	WEDNESDAY	THURSDAY
	1	2	3
7	8	9	10
14	15	16	17
21	22	23	24
28	29	30	

November   2022

FRIDAY	SATURDAY	SUNDAY	Notes
4	5	6	
11	12	13	
18	19	20	
25	26	27	

Shit To Do

_____
_____
_____
_____
_____
_____
_____
_____
_____
_____
_____
_____
_____
_____
_____
_____
_____
_____
_____
_____
_____
_____
_____
_____
_____

Shit To Do

Shit To Do

December

2022

MONTHLY GOALS

MONTHLY SNAPSHOT

TOP PRIORITIES

TASKS & NOTES

Shit to Get Done This Month

TASK/PROJECT	DUE DATE
○	
○	
○	
○	
○	
○	
○	
○	
○	
○	
○	
○	
○	
○	
○	
○	
○	
○	
○	
○	
○	
○	
○	
○	
○	

December 2022

MONDAY	TUESDAY	WEDNESDAY	THURSDAY
29	30	31	1
5	6	7	8
12	13	14	15
19	20	21	22
26	27	28	29

December 2022

FRIDAY	SATURDAY	SUNDAY	Notes
2	3	4	
9	10	11	
16	17	18	
23	24	25	
30	31		

Shit To Do

_____

_____

_____

_____

_____

_____

_____

_____

_____

_____

_____

_____

_____

_____

_____

_____

_____

_____

_____

_____

_____

_____

_____

_____

Shit To Do

Shit To Do

_____

_____

_____

_____

_____

_____

_____

_____

_____

_____

_____

_____

_____

_____

_____

_____

_____

_____

_____

2023

GOALS FOR 2023:

2023

January

MON	TUE	WED	THU	FRI	SAT	SUN
						1
2	3	4	5	6	7	8
9	10	11	12	13	14	15
16	17	18	19	20	21	22
23	24	25	26	27	28	29
30	31					

February

MON	TUE	WED	THU	FRI	SAT	SUN
		1	2	3	4	5
6	7	8	9	10	11	12
13	14	15	16	17	18	19
20	21	22	23	24	25	26
27	28					

March

MON	TUE	WED	THU	FRI	SAT	SUN
		1	2	3	4	5
6	7	8	9	10	11	12
13	14	15	16	17	18	19
20	21	22	23	24	25	26
27	28	29	30	31		

April

MON	TUE	WED	THU	FRI	SAT	SUN
					1	2
3	4	5	6	7	8	9
10	11	12	13	14	15	16
17	18	19	20	21	22	23
24	25	26	27	28	29	30

May

MON	TUE	WED	THU	FRI	SAT	SUN
1	2	3	4	5	6	7
8	9	10	11	12	13	14
15	16	17	18	19	20	21
22	23	24	25	26	27	28
29	30	31				

June

MON	TUE	WED	THU	FRI	SAT	SUN
			1	2	3	4
5	6	7	8	9	10	11
12	13	14	15	16	17	18
19	20	21	22	23	24	25
26	27	28	29	30		

Notes

_____

_____

_____

_____

_____

_____

_____

_____

_____

2023

July

MON	TUE	WED	THU	FRI	SAT	SUN
					1	2
3	4	5	6	7	8	9
10	11	12	13	14	15	16
17	18	19	20	21	22	23
24	25	26	27	28	29	30
31						

August

MON	TUE	WED	THU	FRI	SAT	SUN
	1	2	3	4	5	6
7	8	9	10	11	12	13
14	15	16	17	18	19	20
21	22	23	24	25	26	27
28	29	30	31			

September

MON	TUE	WED	THU	FRI	SAT	SUN
				1	2	3
4	5	6	7	8	9	10
11	12	13	14	15	16	17
18	19	20	21	22	23	24
25	26	27	28	29	30	

October

MON	TUE	WED	THU	FRI	SAT	SUN
						1
2	3	4	5	6	7	8
9	10	11	12	13	14	15
16	17	18	19	20	21	22
23	24	25	26	27	28	29
30	31					

November

MON	TUE	WED	THU	FRI	SAT	SUN
		1	2	3	4	5
6	7	8	9	10	11	12
13	14	15	16	17	18	19
20	21	22	23	24	25	26
27	28	29	30			

December

MON	TUE	WED	THU	FRI	SAT	SUN
				1	2	3
4	5	6	7	8	9	10
11	12	13	14	15	16	17
18	19	20	21	22	23	24
25	26	27	28	29	30	31

Notes

January

2023

MONTHLY SNAPSHOT

MONTHLY GOALS

TOP PRIORITIES

TASKS & NOTES

Shit to Get Done This Month

TASK/PROJECT	DUE DATE
○	
○	
○	
○	
○	
○	
○	
○	
○	
○	
○	
○	
○	
○	
○	
○	
○	
○	
○	
○	
○	
○	
○	
○	
○	

January 2023

MONDAY	TUESDAY	WEDNESDAY	THURSDAY
2	3	4	5
9	10	11	12
16	17	18	19
23	24	25	26
30	31		

January 2023

FRIDAY	SATURDAY	SUNDAY	Notes
		1	_____
			_____
			_____
6	7	8	_____
			_____
			_____
13	14	15	_____
			_____
			_____
20	21	22	_____
			_____
			_____
27	28	29	_____
			_____
			_____
			_____
			_____

Shit To Do

_____

_____

_____

_____

_____

_____

_____

_____

_____

_____

_____

_____

_____

_____

_____

_____

_____

_____

_____

_____

_____

_____

Shit To Do

_____

_____

_____

_____

_____

_____

_____

_____

_____

_____

_____

_____

_____

_____

_____

_____

_____

_____

_____

_____

_____

_____

_____

Shit To Do

_____

_____

_____

_____

_____

_____

_____

_____

_____

_____

_____

_____

_____

_____

_____

_____

_____

_____

_____

_____

February

2023

MONTHLY GOALS

MONTHLY SNAPSHOT

TOP PRIORITIES

TASKS & NOTES

Shit to Get Done This Month

TASK/PROJECT	DUE DATE
○	
○	
○	
○	
○	
○	
○	
○	
○	
○	
○	
○	
○	
○	
○	
○	
○	
○	
○	
○	
○	
○	
○	
○	

February 2023

MONDAY	TUESDAY	WEDNESDAY	THURSDAY
		1	2
6	7	8	9
13	14	15	16
20	21	22	23
27	28		

February

2023

FRIDAY	SATURDAY	SUNDAY	Notes
3	4	5	
10	11	12	
17	18	19	
24	25	26	

Shit To Do

Shit To Do

Shit To Do

_____

_____

_____

_____

_____

_____

_____

_____

_____

_____

_____

_____

_____

_____

_____

_____

_____

_____

_____

_____

_____

_____

March

2023

MONTHLY GOALS

MONTHLY SNAPSHOT

TOP PRIORITIES

TASKS & NOTES

Shit to Get Done This Month

TASK/PROJECT	DUE DATE
○	
○	
○	
○	
○	
○	
○	
○	
○	
○	
○	
○	
○	
○	
○	
○	
○	
○	
○	
○	
○	
○	
○	
○	

March 2023

MONDAY	TUESDAY	WEDNESDAY	THURSDAY
		1	2
6	7	8	9
13	14	15	16
20	21	22	23
27	28	29	30

March 2023

FRIDAY	SATURDAY	SUNDAY	Notes
	3	4	5
10	11	12	
17	18	19	
24	25	26	
31			

Shit To Do

_____

_____

_____

_____

_____

_____

_____

_____

_____

_____

_____

_____

_____

_____

_____

_____

_____

_____

_____

_____

Shit To Do

_____

_____

_____

_____

_____

_____

_____

_____

_____

_____

_____

_____

_____

_____

_____

_____

_____

_____

_____

_____

Shit To Do

_____

_____

_____

_____

_____

_____

_____

_____

_____

_____

_____

_____

_____

_____

_____

_____

_____

_____

_____

_____

2023

MONTHLY GOALS

MONTHLY SNAPSHOT

TOP PRIORITIES

TASKS & NOTES

Shit to Get Done This Month

TASK/PROJECT	DUE DATE
○	
○	
○	
○	
○	
○	
○	
○	
○	
○	
○	
○	
○	
○	
○	
○	
○	
○	
○	
○	
○	
○	
○	
○	

April
2023

MONDAY	TUESDAY	WEDNESDAY	THURSDAY
3	4	5	6
10	11	12	13
17	18	19	20
24	25	26	27

April 2023

FRIDAY	SATURDAY	SUNDAY	Notes
		1	2
7	8	9	
14	15	16	
21	22	23	
28	29	30	

Shit To Do

_____

_____

_____

_____

_____

_____

_____

_____

_____

_____

_____

_____

_____

_____

_____

_____

_____

_____

_____

_____

_____

_____

_____

Shit To Do

Shit To Do

May

2023

MONTHLY GOALS

MONTHLY SNAPSHOT

TOP PRIORITIES

TASKS & NOTES

Shit to Get Done This Month

TASK/PROJECT	DUE DATE
○	
○	
○	
○	
○	
○	
○	
○	
○	
○	
○	
○	
○	
○	
○	
○	
○	
○	
○	
○	
○	
○	
○	
○	
○	

May

2023

MONDAY	TUESDAY	WEDNESDAY	THURSDAY
1	2	3	4
8	9	10	11
15	16	17	18
22	23	24	25
29	30	31	

May

2023

FRIDAY	SATURDAY	SUNDAY	Notes
5	6	7	
12	13	14	
19	20	21	
26	27	28	

Shit To Do

_____
_____
_____
_____
_____
_____
_____
_____
_____
_____
_____
_____
_____
_____
_____
_____
_____
_____
_____
_____
_____

Shit To Do

_____

_____

_____

_____

_____

_____

_____

_____

_____

_____

_____

_____

_____

_____

_____

_____

_____

_____

_____

Shit To Do

_____
_____
_____
_____
_____
_____
_____
_____
_____
_____
_____
_____
_____
_____
_____
_____
_____
_____
_____
_____
_____
_____

June

2023

MONTHLY SNAPSHOT

TOP PRIORITIES

TASKS & NOTES

Shit to Get Done This Month

TASK/PROJECT	DUE DATE
○	
○	
○	
○	
○	
○	
○	
○	
○	
○	
○	
○	
○	
○	
○	
○	
○	
○	
○	
○	
○	
○	
○	
○	
○	

June

2023

MONDAY	TUESDAY	WEDNESDAY	THURSDAY
			1
5	6	7	8
12	13	14	15
19	20	21	22
26	27	28	29

June 2023

FRIDAY	SATURDAY	SUNDAY	Notes
2	3	4	
9	10	11	
16	17	18	
23	24	25	
30			

Shit To Do

Shit To Do

_____

_____

_____

_____

_____

_____

_____

_____

_____

_____

_____

_____

_____

_____

_____

_____

_____

_____

_____

_____

_____

_____

_____

_____

Shit To Do

_____
_____
_____
_____
_____
_____
_____
_____
_____
_____
_____
_____
_____
_____
_____
_____
_____
_____
_____
_____
_____
_____

July

2023

MONTHLY GOALS

MONTHLY SNAPSHOT

TOP PRIORITIES

TASKS & NOTES

Shit to Get Done This Month

TASK/PROJECT	DUE DATE
○	
○	
○	
○	
○	
○	
○	
○	
○	
○	
○	
○	
○	
○	
○	
○	
○	
○	
○	
○	
○	
○	
○	
○	
○	

July
2023

MONDAY	TUESDAY	WEDNESDAY	THURSDAY
3	4	5	6
10	11	12	13
17	18	19	20
24	25	26	27
31			

July

2023

FRIDAY	SATURDAY	SUNDAY	Notes
		1	_____
		2	_____
7	8	9	_____
14	15	16	_____
21	22	23	_____
28	29	30	_____

Shit To Do

_____
_____
_____
_____
_____
_____
_____
_____
_____
_____
_____
_____
_____
_____
_____
_____
_____
_____
_____
_____
_____
_____
_____

Shit To Do

Shit To Do

August

2023

MONTHLY GOALS

MONTHLY SNAPSHOT

TOP PRIORITIES

TASKS & NOTES

Shit to Get Done This Month

TASK/PROJECT	DUE DATE
○	
○	
○	
○	
○	
○	
○	
○	
○	
○	
○	
○	
○	
○	
○	
○	
○	
○	
○	
○	
○	
○	
○	
○	
○	

August 2023

MONDAY	TUESDAY	WEDNESDAY	THURSDAY
	1	2	3
7	8	9	10
14	15	16	17
21	22	23	24
28	29	30	31

August 2023

FRIDAY	SATURDAY	SUNDAY	Notes
4	5	6	
11	12	13	
18	19	20	
25	26	27	

Shit To Do

_____
_____
_____
_____
_____
_____
_____
_____
_____
_____
_____
_____
_____
_____
_____
_____
_____
_____
_____
_____
_____
_____
_____
_____

Shit To Do

_____

_____

_____

_____

_____

_____

_____

_____

_____

_____

_____

_____

_____

_____

_____

_____

_____

_____

_____

_____

Shit To Do

_____
_____
_____
_____
_____
_____
_____
_____
_____
_____
_____
_____
_____
_____
_____
_____
_____
_____
_____
_____

September

2023

MONTHLY GOALS

MONTHLY SNAPSHOT

TOP PRIORITIES

TASKS & NOTES

Shit to Get Done This Month

TASK/PROJECT	DUE DATE
⭕	
⭕	
⭕	
⭕	
⭕	
⭕	
⭕	
⭕	
⭕	
⭕	
⭕	
⭕	
⭕	
⭕	
⭕	
⭕	
⭕	
⭕	
⭕	
⭕	
⭕	
⭕	
⭕	
⭕	

September

2023

MONDAY	TUESDAY	WEDNESDAY	THURSDAY
4	5	6	7
11	12	13	14
18	19	20	21
25	26	27	28

September

2023

FRIDAY	SATURDAY	SUNDAY	Notes
	1	2	3
8	9	10	
15	16	17	
22	23	24	
29	30		

Shit To Do

_____

_____

_____

_____

_____

_____

_____

_____

_____

_____

_____

_____

_____

_____

_____

_____

_____

_____

_____

_____

Shit To Do

Shit To Do

_____
_____
_____
_____
_____
_____
_____
_____
_____
_____
_____
_____
_____
_____
_____
_____
_____
_____
_____
_____
_____
_____
_____
_____

October

2023

MONTHLY GOALS

MONTHLY SNAPSHOT

TOP PRIORITIES

TASKS & NOTES

Shit to Get Done This Month

TASK/PROJECT	DUE DATE
○	
○	
○	
○	
○	
○	
○	
○	
○	
○	
○	
○	
○	
○	
○	
○	
○	
○	
○	
○	
○	
○	
○	

October 2023

MONDAY	TUESDAY	WEDNESDAY	THURSDAY
2	3	4	5
9	10	11	12
16	17	18	19
23	24	25	26
30	31		

October 2023

FRIDAY	SATURDAY	SUNDAY	Notes
		1	
6	7	8	
13	14	15	
20	21	22	
27	28	29	

Shit To Do

Shit To Do

Shit To Do

_____
_____
_____
_____
_____
_____
_____
_____
_____
_____
_____
_____
_____
_____
_____
_____
_____
_____
_____
_____
_____
_____

November

2023

MONTHLY SNAPSHOT

TOP PRIORITIES

TASKS & NOTES

Shit to Get Done This Month

TASK/PROJECT	DUE DATE
○	
○	
○	
○	
○	
○	
○	
○	
○	
○	
○	
○	
○	
○	
○	
○	
○	
○	
○	
○	
○	
○	
○	
○	
○	

November

2023

MONDAY	TUESDAY	WEDNESDAY	THURSDAY
		1	2
6	7	8	9
13	14	15	16
20	21	22	23
27	28	29	30

November

2023

FRIDAY	SATURDAY	SUNDAY	Notes
3	4	5	_____
			_____
10	11	12	_____
			_____
			_____
17	18	19	_____
			_____
			_____
24	25	26	_____
			_____
			_____
			_____
			_____
			_____
			_____
			_____
			_____

Shit To Do

Shit To Do

_____
_____
_____
_____
_____
_____
_____
_____
_____
_____
_____
_____
_____
_____
_____
_____
_____
_____
_____
_____
_____
_____

Shit To Do

_____

_____

_____

_____

_____

_____

_____

_____

_____

_____

_____

_____

_____

_____

_____

_____

_____

_____

_____

_____

_____

_____

December

2023

MONTHLY GOALS

MONTHLY SNAPSHOT

TOP PRIORITIES

TASKS & NOTES

Shit to Get Done This Month

TASK/PROJECT	DUE DATE
○	
○	
○	
○	
○	
○	
○	
○	
○	
○	
○	
○	
○	
○	
○	
○	
○	
○	
○	
○	
○	
○	
○	
○	
○	
○	

December 2023

MONDAY	TUESDAY	WEDNESDAY	THURSDAY
4	5	6	7
11	12	13	14
18	19	20	21
25	26	27	28

December

2023

FRIDAY	SATURDAY	SUNDAY	Notes
	1	2	3
	8	9	10
	15	16	17
	22	23	24
	29	30	31

Shit To Do

_____
_____
_____
_____
_____
_____
_____
_____
_____
_____
_____
_____
_____
_____
_____
_____
_____
_____
_____
_____
_____
_____

Shit To Do

_____

_____

_____

_____

_____

_____

_____

_____

_____

_____

_____

_____

_____

_____

_____

_____

_____

_____

_____

_____

_____

_____

Shit To Do